E S T A T E   P U B L I

C000257932

BURTON UPON

· SWADLINCOTE · ASHBY-DE-L.

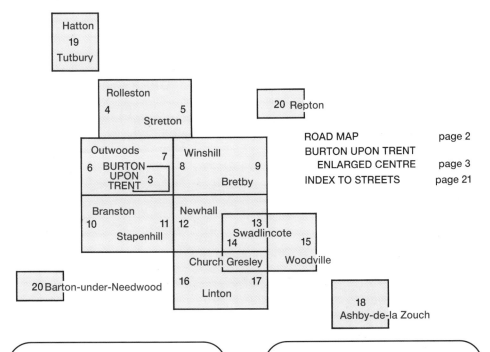

Hatton 19 Tutbury	
Rolleston 4 5 Stretton	20 Repton
	ROAD MAP — page 2
	BURTON UPON TRENT
	ENLARGED CENTRE — page 3
	INDEX TO STREETS — page 21

Outwoods 6   7
BURTON UPON TRENT 3

Winshill 8   9
Bretby

Branston 10   11
Stapenhill

Newhall 12   13
Swadlincote 14   15
Woodville

20 Barton-under-Needwood

Church Gresley 16   17
Linton

18
Ashby-de-la Zouch

Every effort has been made to verify the accuracy of information in this book but the publishers cannot accept responsibility for expense or loss caused by any error or omission. Information that will be of assistance to the user of the maps will be welcomed.

The representation of a road, track or footpath on the maps in this atlas is no evidence of the existence of a right of way.

One-way Street	→
Car Park	🅿
Place of Worship	✚
Post Office	●
Public Convenience	☉
Pedestrianized	▨

Scale of street plans 4 inches to 1 mile
Unless otherwise stated

Street plans prepared and published by ESTATE PUBLICATIONS, Bridewell House, TENTERDEN, KENT. The Publishers acknowledge the co-operation of the local authorities of towns represented in this atlas.

Ordnance Survey® This product includes mapping data licensed from Ordnance Survey® with the permission of the Controller of Her Majesty's Stationery Office.

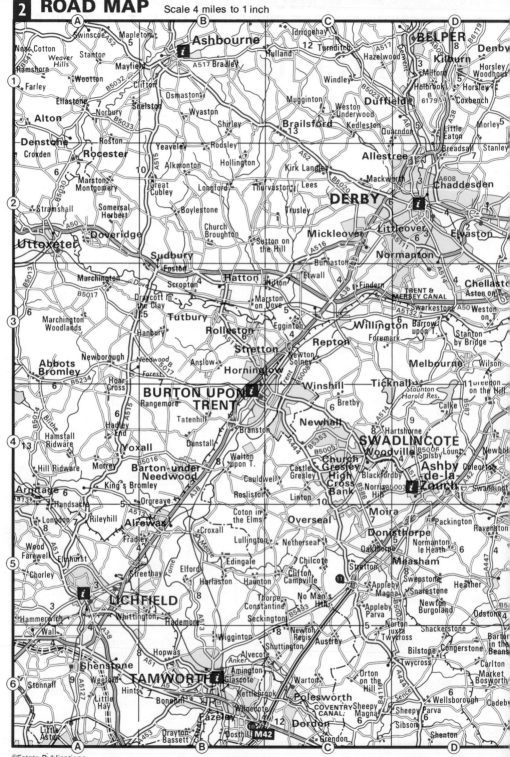

©Estate Publications

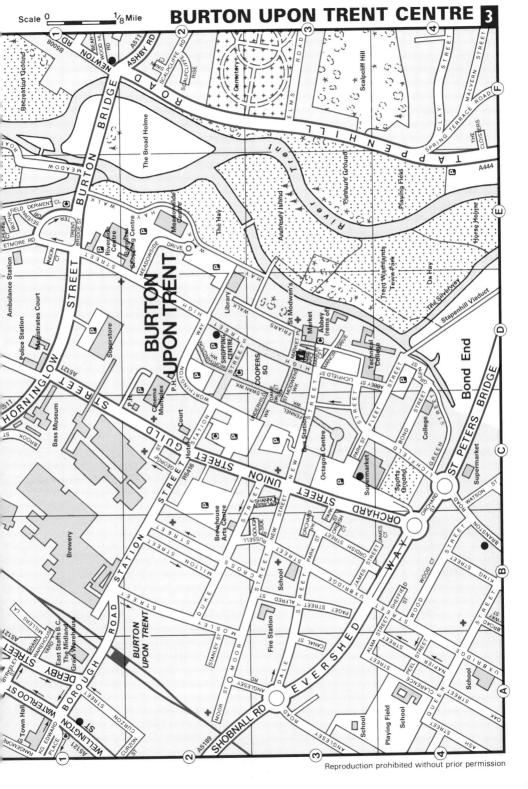

Scale 0 — 1/8 Mile

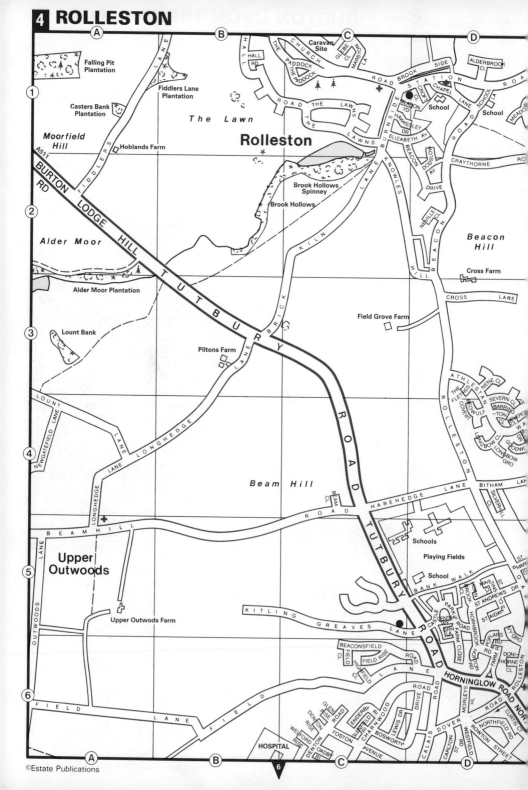

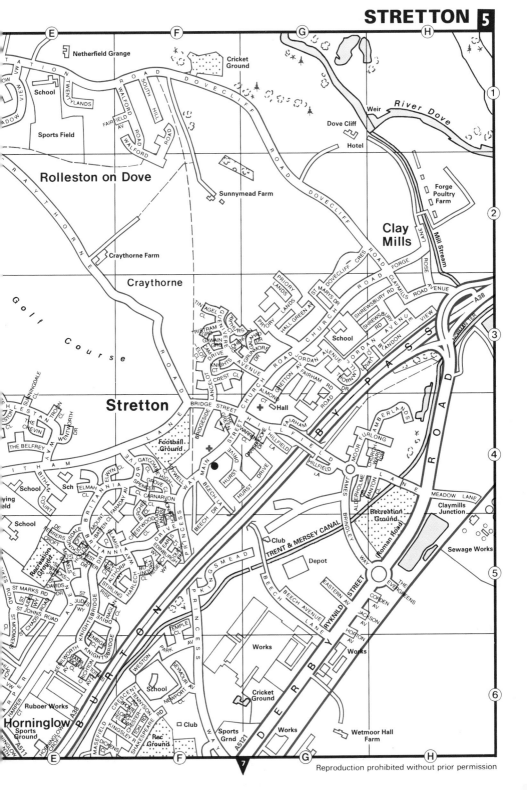

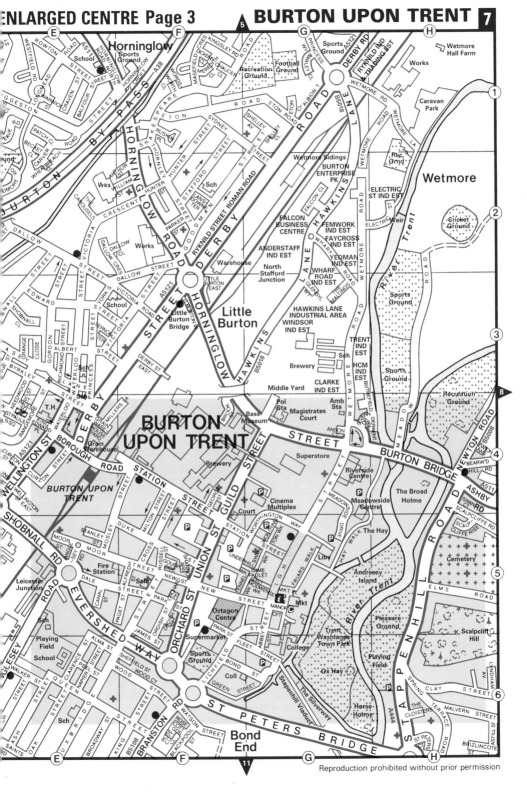

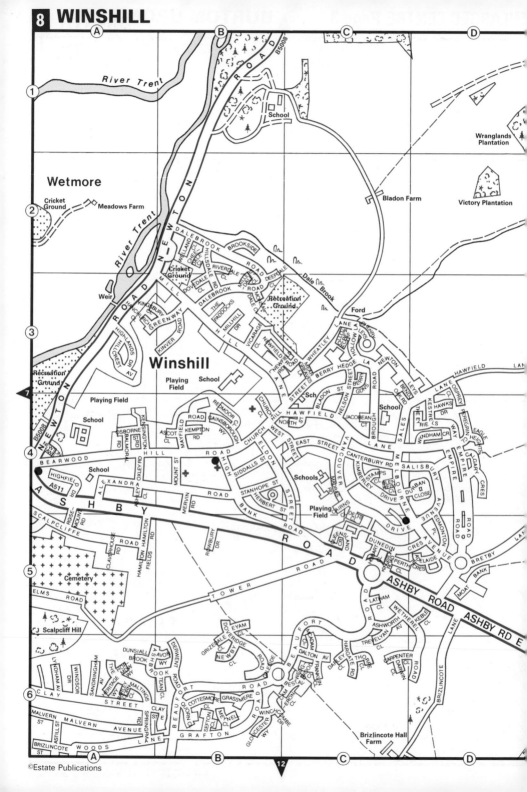

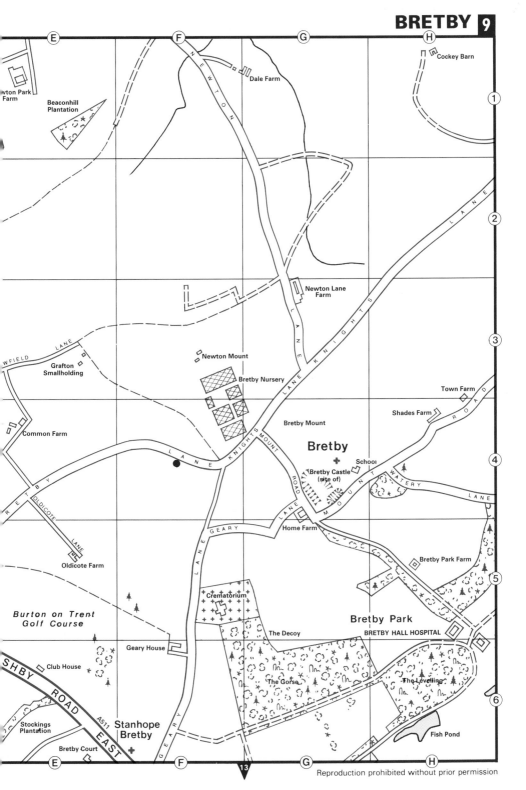

Cockey Barn

Dale Farm

Newton Park Farm

Beaconhill Plantation

Newton Lane Farm

WFIELD LANE

Grafton Smallholding

Newton Mount

Bretby Nursery

Town Farm

Shades Farm

Common Farm

Bretby Mount

Bretby

School

Bretby Castle (site of)

LANE

KNIGHTS

MOUNT

BRETBY

OLDICOTE LANE

WATERY LANE

GEARY LANE

Home Farm

Oldicote Farm

Bretby Park Farm

Crematorium

Burton on Trent Golf Course

The Decoy

Bretby Park

BRETBY HALL HOSPITAL

Geary House

Club House

The Gorse

The Levelling

SHBY ROAD EAST

A511

Stockings Plantation

Stanhope Bretby

Bretby Court

Fish Pond

10 BRANSTON

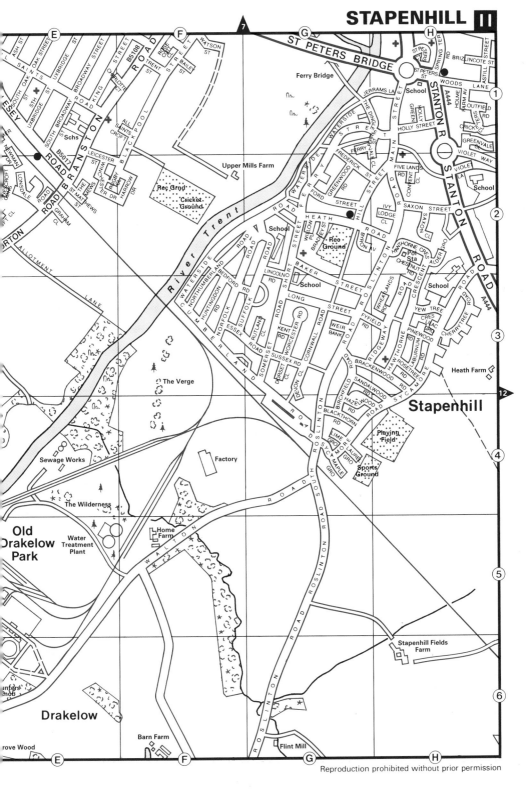

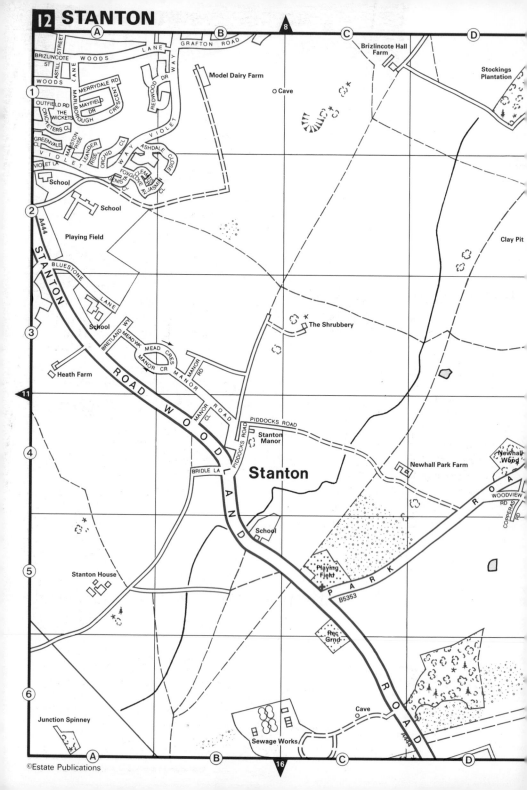

STANTON

Model Dairy Farm

Brizlincote Hall Farm

Stockings Plantation

○ Cave

BRIZLINCOTE ST
ASTILL ST
BRIZLINCOTE WOODS
WOODS
LANE
LANE
GRAFTON ROAD
REDWOOD DR
MERRYDALE RD
MARLBOROUGH
MAYFIELD DR
CRESCENT
MARSTON RISE
OUTFIELD RD
THE WICKETS
CRICKETERS CL
GREENVALE CL
VIOLET
ORCHARD CL
VIOLET WAY
ASHDALE CLOSE
VIOLET LA
GENISTA CL
FOXGLOVE
CLEMATIS CL
JASMIN CL
School

School

Playing Field

A444

STANTON

Clay Pit

BLUESTONE LANE

School

Heath Farm

BRETLAND MEADOW
MEAD CRES
MANOR CR
MANOR CL
MANOR RD
MANOR
ROAD

ROAD WOODLAND

The Shrubbery

PIDDOCKS ROAD

PIDDOCKS ROAD

Stanton Manor

BRIDLE LA

Stanton

Newhall Park Farm

Newhall Wood

WOODVIEW RD

COPPERAS RD

PARK ROAD

School

Stanton House

Playing Field

B5353

Rec Grnd

Junction Spinney

Cave

Sewage Works

A444 ROAD

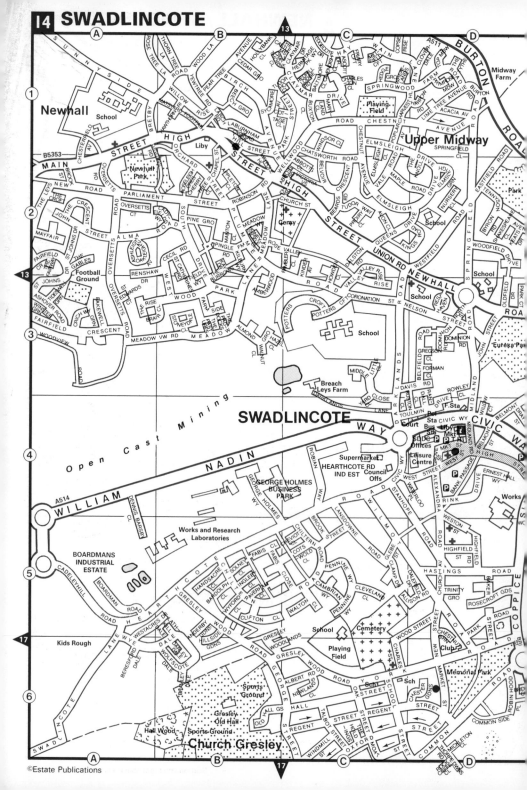

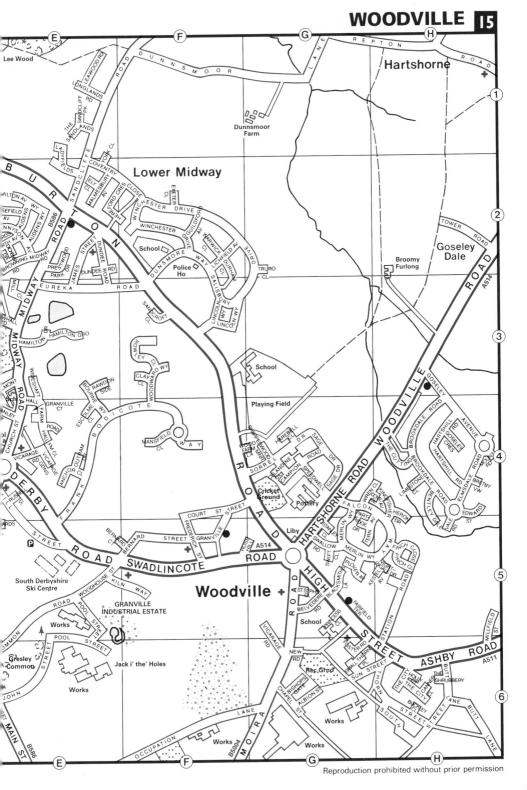

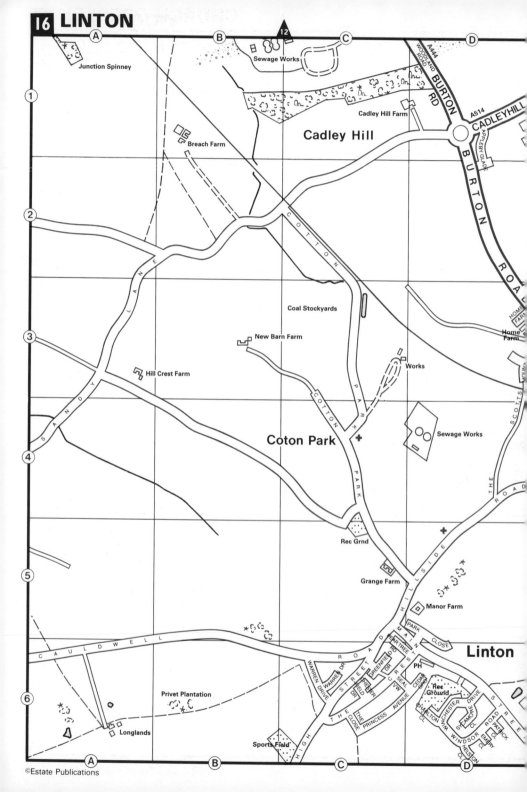

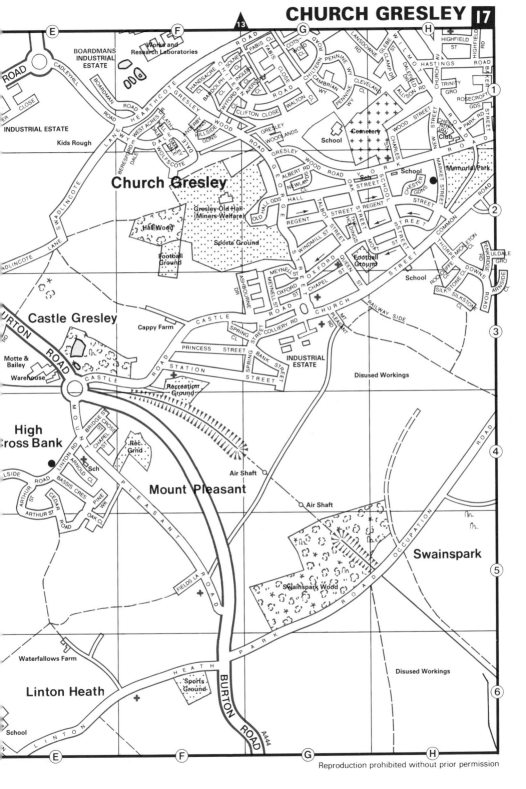

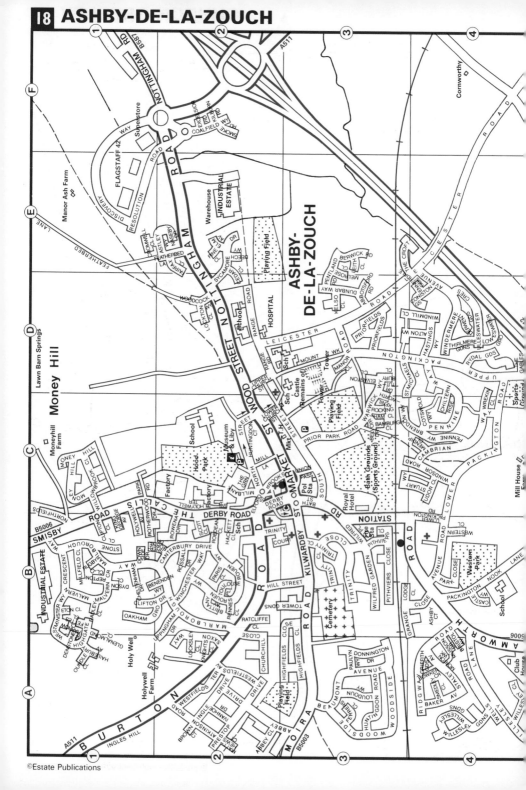

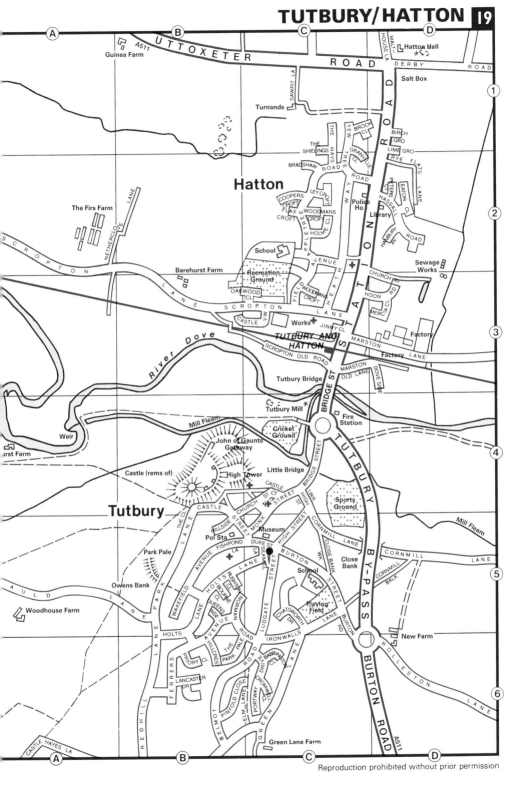

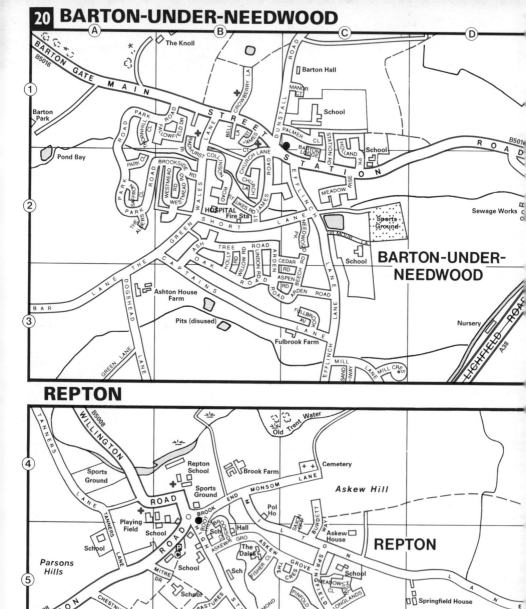

BARTON-UNDER-NEEDWOOD

REPTON

Eton Clo. DE14 7 G1
Eton Rd. DE14 7 F1
Eureka Rd. DE11 15 E3
Evershed Way. DE14 3 A3
Exeter Clo. DE11 15 F2
Eyam Clo. DE15 8 B5

Fabis Clo. DE11 14 B5
Fairfield Av. DE13 5 F1
Fairfield Cres. DE11 14 A3
Fairfield Ter. DE11 15 G6
Fairham Clo. DE11 5 G4
Fairham Rd. DE13 5 G3
Fairway. DE14 10 D3
Falcon Clo. DE14 7 G2
Falcon Way. DE11 15 G4
Faldo Clo. DE14 10 D3
Faraday Av. DE13 5 F4
Farm Clo. DE113 4 D5
Farm Rd. DE13 4 D6
Farm Side. DE11 4 B1
Faversham Rd. DE13 6 C1
Fennel Walk. DE14 3 C3
Ferry Clo. DE11 11 G2
Festival Rd. DE14 10 B2
Fiddlers La. DE13 4 A2
Field Clo. DE13 4 C6
Field La. DE13 4 A6
Field Rise. DE13 4 C6
Field Way. DE11 14 B3
Finch Clo. DE11 15 H5
First Av. DE14 10 B2
Five Lands Rd. DE15 11 H2
Flatts Clo. DE13 7 E1
Fleet St. DE14 3 C4
Fontwell Rd. DE14 10 C2
Ford Clo. DE15 11 G2
Forest Rd. DE13 6 A3
Forge La. DE13 5 H2
Forman Clo. DE11 14 D3
Foster Rd. DE11 15 G6
Foston Av. DE13 6 D1
Fox Clo. DE14 10 D1
Foxglove Av. DE11 12 A2
Frank Bodicote Way. DE11 15 E4
Franklin Clo. DE15 8 C6
Frederick St, Stapenhill. DE11 11 G2
Frederick St, Woodville. DE11 15 F5
Friars Walk. DE14 3 D3
Friary Croft. DE11 14 C1
Fyfield Rd. DE15 11 G3

Gainsborough Way. DE15 8 B4
Galahad Dri. DE13 5 G3
Gartan Rd. DE14 10 D2
Gatcombe Clo. DE13 5 F4
Gawain Gro. DE13 5 F3
Geary La. DE15 9 F6
Genista Clo. DE15 12 A2
George Holmes Way. DE11 14 B4
George St, Burton on T. DE14 3 C2
George St, Church Gresley. DE11 14 B6
Glamis Clo. DE13 5 E5
Glebe Clo. DE13 4 C1
Glebe St. DE12 14 C5
Glen Rise. DE13 4 C6
Glencroft Clo. DE14 11 E2
Gleneagles Dri. DE13 4 D4
Glenfield Rise. DE13 4 C6
Glensyl Way. DE14 7 G3
Gloucester Way. DE15 8 B6
Goodman St. DE14 7 F2
Goodwood Clo. DE13 4 D4
Gordon St. DE14 7 E3
Goseley Av. DE11 15 H3
Goseley Cres. DE11 15 H4
Gough Side. DE11 3 B3
Grafton Rd. DE15 8 E2
Graham Clo. DE14 11 E2
Grain Warehouse Yd. DE14 3 A1
Grange Clo. DE14 7 E3
Grange Rd. DE11 13 E4
Grange St. DE14 6 D4
Granville Ct. DE11 15 E4
Granville St. DE14 15 F5
Grassmere. DE15 8 B6
Green La. DE13 4 D5
Green St. DE14 3 C4
Greenfield Dri. DE12 16 C6
Greenlands DE11 13 G2

Greenvale Clo. DE15 11 H1
Greenway. DE15 8 A3
Greenwood St. DE15 11 G2
Gregson Clo. DE11 14 D3
Gresley Wood Rd. DE11 14 B5
Gresley Woodlands. DE11 14 B6
Gretton Av. DE13 5 G3
Grizedale Clo. DE15 8 B6
Grove St. DE11 14 D4
Grunmore Dri. DE13 5 G3
Guenivere Av. DE13 5 F3
Guild St. DE14 3 C2
Guildford Av. DE11 15 F2

Halcyon.Ct. DE14 6 D3
Halcyon Way. DE14 6 D3
Hall Farm Clo. DE11 15 E4
Hall Farm Rd. DE11 15 E4
Hall Green Av. DE13 5 G3
Hall Rd. DE13 4 B1
Hall St. DE11 14 C6
Hamilton Dri. DE11 15 E3
Hamilton Gro. DE11 15 E3
Hamilton Fields. DE15 8 A5
Hamilton Rd. DE15 8 A5
Hanchurch Clo. DE15 8 A3
Handsacre Clo. DE11 14 B5
Harbury St. DE13 6 D1
Harcourt Rd. DE14 10 B1
Harebell Clo. DE15 12 A1
Harehedge La. DE13 4 C4
Hargate Rd. DE15 8 C6
Harlaxton St. DE13 6 D1
Harlech Way. DE13 5 F5
Harper Av. DE13 5 E6
Harper Ct. DE13 5 E6
Harrison Clo. DE14 10 D1
Harrow Dri. DE14 11 F2
Harrow Rd. DE11 14 D1
Hartshill Rd. DE11 15 H4
Hartshorne Rd. DE11 15 G5
Harvest Hill. DE11 14 C1
Harvey Rd. DE14 10 D1
Harwood Av. DE14 10 B2
Hastings Rd. DE11 14 D5
Hawfield La. DE15 8 C4
Hawfield La. DE15 8 D3
Hawkesley Dri. DE13 4 C1
Hawkins La. DE14 7 G2
Hawks Dri. DE15 8 D4
Hawthorn Cres. DE11 11 H2
Hawthorn Rise. DE11 14 B1
Hay Wain La. DE11 14 C1
Hay Walk. DE14 3 D2
Haydock Clo. DE14 10 C2
Hazel Clo. DE12 14 B4
Hazelwood Rd. DE15 11 G4
Hearthcote Rd. DE11 14 A5
Heath Rd. DE15 11 G2
Hedge Gro. DE11 14 C1
Helston Clo. DE12 16 D6
Herbert St. DE15 8 B4
Hereford Cres. DE11 15 E2
Heritage Way. DE15 8 A6
Hermitage Parkway. DE11 13 G2
Heron Dri. DE11 15 H4
Higgins Rd. DE11 14 A1
Higgott Clo. DE14 10 D1
High Bank Rd. DE15 8 B4
High St, Burton on T. DE14 3 D3
High St, Linton. DE12 16 C6
High St, Newhall. DE11 14 B1
High St, Swadlincote. DE11 14 D4
High St, Woodville. DE11 15 G5
Highcroft Dri. DE14 6 C3
Highfield Clo. DE13 4 C6
Highfield Dri. DE15 8 A4
Highfield Rd. DE11 14 D5
Highfield St. DE11 14 D5
Highgrove Clo. DE13 5 F4
Highlands Dri. DE15 8 A3
Hill St, Newhall. DE11 14 B1
Hill St, Stapenhill. DE11 11 G2
Hill St, Swadlincote. DE11 15 E4
Hillcrest Av. DE15 8 A3
Hillfield La. DE13 5 G4
Hillsdale Rd. DE15 8 B2
Hillside Gdns. DE15 14 B6
Hillside Rd. DE11 17 E4
Hilton Clo. DE15 13 G2
Hobart Clo. DE15 8 C5

Hollow Cres. DE15 8 C3
Hollow La. DE15 8 C3
Holly Ct. DE11 15 H6
Holly Green. DE15 11 H1
Holly St. DE15 11 H1
Hollybank Clo. DE15 13 G2
Hollyhock Way. DE14 10 B3
Holme Farm Av. DE15 11 H1
Home Farm Ct. DE11 16 D3
Honeysuckle Clo. DE11 14 B2
Hopmeadow Way. DE15 8 A6
Hornbrook Clo. DE13 4 D5
Hornbrook Rd. DE13 4 D5
Horninglow Ct. DE13 7 F1
Horninglow Rd. DE14 7 F1
Horninglow Rd Nth. DE13 4 D6
Horninglow St. DE14 3 C1
Horton Av. DE13 5 G5
Horton Rd. DE13 4 C4
Howden Clo. DE11 13 G4
Hunter St. DE14 7 F1
Huntingdon Rd. DE15 11 F3
Hurst Dri. DE13 5 F4
Hylton Clo. DE14 10 C2

Ibstock St. DE13 6 D1

INDUSTRIAL & RETAIL:
Anderstaff Ind Est. DE14 7 G2
Boardmans Ind Est. DE11 14 A5
Bretby Business Pk. DE11 13 F1
Burton Enterprise Pk. DE14 7 G2
Centrum Business Pk. DE14 10 B1
Clarke Ind Est. DE14 7 G3
Electric St Ind Est. DE14 7 H2
Falcon Business Centre. DE14 7 G2
Faycross Ind Est. DE14 7 G2
Femwork Ind Est. DE14 7 G2
George Holmes Business Pk. DE11 14 B4
Granville Ind Est. DE11 15 E5
Hawkins Lane Ind Area. DE14 7 G3
HCM Ind Est. DE14 7 G3
Hearthcote Rd Ind Est. DE11 14 C4
Ryknild Ind & Trading Est. DE14 7 G1
Trent Ind Est. DE14 7 G3
Wharf Rd Ind Est. DE14 7 G2
Windsor Ind Est. DE14 7 G3
Yeoman Ind Est. DE14 7 G2
Ingleby Clo. DE14 14 B5
Ivy Gro. DE13 4 D5
Ivy Lodge Clo. DE15 11 H2

Jacklin Clo. DE14 10 D3
Jackson Av. DE13 5 G5
Jacobean Ct. DE15 8 C4
James Brindley Way. DE13 5 G4
James Ct. DE14 3 B4
James St, Burton. DE14 3 B3
James St, Swadlincote. DE11 15 E2
Jasmin Clo. DE15 12 A2
Jennings Way. DE14 6 D4
Jerrams La. DE15 11 H1
John St, Church Gresley. DE11 15 E6
John St, Newhall. DE11 14 A2
John St, Swadlincote. DE11 14 D3
Jordan Av. DE13 5 G3

Kay Dri. DE11 14 B2
Keats Dri. DE11 14 D2
Keble Clo. DE15 8 D5
Kedleston Clo. DE13 5 E4
Kempton Rd. DE15 8 B4
Kenilworth Av. DE13 5 E6
Kensington Rd. DE15 8 A4
Kent Rd. DE11 11 G3
Kestrel Av. DE11 15 H5
Kestrels Way. DE15 8 D4
Kilburn Way. DE11 14 B2
Kiln Way. DE11 15 E5
Kimberley Dri. DE15 8 C4

Kinder Av. DE11 13 G4
King Edward Pl. DE14 3 A1
King St. DE14 3 B4
Kingfisher Av. DE11 15 H4
Kings Rd. DE14 14 C2
Kingsbury Clo. DE15 8 A3
Kingsdale Croft. DE13 5 E5
Kingsley Rd. DE14 7 F1
Kingsmead. DE13 5 F5
Kingston Rd. DE15 8 C5
Kingsway. DE14 10 D2
Kinver Rd. DE15 8 B3
Kitling Greaves La. DE14 4 B5
Knights Clo. DE13 5 F3
Knights La. DE15 9 F4
Knightsbridge Dri. DE13 5 E5
Knowles Hill. DE13 4 C2

Laburnham Rd, Swadlincote. DE11 14 B1
Laburnum Rd, Stapenhill. DE15 11 H3
Ladyfields. DE11 15 E2
Ladyfields Way. DE11 14 B2
Ladywell Clo. DE15 5 F4
Lancelot Clo. DE13 5 F3
Langer Clo. DE14 10 D3
Lansdowne Rd, Branston. DE14 10 C3
Lansdowne Rd, Newhall. DE11 14 C4
Lansdowne Ter. DE14 7 F2
Larch Rd. DE11 14 B1
Latham St. DE15 8 C5
Lathkill Dale. DE11 14 B5
Laurel Gro. DE11 13 G2
Lawns Dri. DE11 13 G2
Leamington Rd. DE14 10 B2
Leander Rise. DE15 12 A2
Leawood Rd. DE11 15 E1
Leicester St. DE14 11 E1
Lewis Dri. DE13 4 C6
Lichfield Av. DE11 15 F2
Lichfield Rd. DE11 10 A4
Lichfield St. DE14 3 C4
Lilac Gro. DE11 11 H3
Lime Gro. DE15 11 G4
Lime Tree Av. DE11 14 D1
Limestone Clo. DE11 15 H4
Lincoln Rd. DE15 11 G2
Lincoln Way. DE11 15 F3
Lingfield Rd. DE14 10 C2
Linton Heath. DE12 17 E6
Linton Rd. DE12 17 E4
Little Clo. DE11 14 C2
Little Burton East. DE14 7 F3
Little Burton West. DE14 7 F3
Lodge Hill. DE11 4 A2
Lohengrin Ct. DE13 5 F3
Long St. DE15 11 G3
Longbow Dri. DE13 4 D4
Longbow Gro. DE13 4 D4
Longfellow Clo. DE14 5 F6
Longhedge La. DE13 4 A4
Longlands Rd. DE11 15 E1
Longmead Rd. DE13 7 E1
Lonsdale Rd. DE14 11 E2
Lordswell Rd. DE14 6 B3
Lount La. DE13 4 A4
Lovatt Clo. DE13 5 G3
Lower Outwoods Rd. DE13 6 C2
Lyndham Av. DE15 8 A6
Lyne Ct. DE14 6 D4
Lynwood Rd. DE14 10 B2

McAdam Clo. DE15 8 C5
Mackworth Clo. DE11 13 G2
Madras Rd. DE15 8 C5
Main St, Branston. DE14 10 A3
Main St, Church Gresley. DE11 15 E6
Main St, Linton. DE12 16 C5
Main St, Newhall. DE11 14 A2
Main St, Stapenhill. DE15 11 H2
Main St, Stretton. DE13 5 F4
Malmesbury Av. DE11 15 E2
Malvern Av. DE15 8 A6
Malvern St. DE15 7 H6
Manor Clo. DE15 12 B4
Manor Cres. DE15 12 A3
Manor Croft. DE4 3 D3
Manor Dri. DE14 3 D3
Manor Rd. DE15 12 B3
Mansfield Clo. DE11 15 F4

Manton Clo, Stretton. DE13 5 H4
Manton Clo, Swadlincote. DE11 14 B2
Maple Gro. DE15 11 G4
Maple Rd. DE11 14 C2
Maple Way. DE14 10 C2
Market Pl. DE14 3 D3
Market St, Church Gresley. DE11 14 D6
Market St, Swadlincote. DE11 14 D4
Marlborough Cres. DE15 12 A1
Marlow Dri. DE14 10 D1
Marston La. DE13 4 C1
Marston Rise. DE15 12 A1
Maryland Clo. DE11 14 C1
Masefield Av. DE11 15 E2
Masefield Cres. DE14 7 F1
Matsyard Footpath. DE11 14 B1
Mayfair. DE11 14 A2
Mayfield Dri. DE11 12 A1
Mayfield Rd. DE15 8 B4
Maypole Hill. DE11 14 B2
Mead Cres. DE15 12 A3
Mead Walk. DE15 12 A3
Meadow La, Newhall. DE11 14 B2
Meadow La, Stretton. DE13 5 H4
Meadow Rd. DE11 3 E1
Meadow View. DE13 4 D1
Meadow View Rd. DE11 14 A3
Meadow Way. DE11 14 B2
Meadowside Dri. DE14 3 E2
Mear Greaves La. DE15 8 C3
Melbourne Av. DE15 8 C4
Mellor Rd. DE14 10 D2
Meredith Clo. DE14 7 F1
Merlin Cres. DE14 10 B2
Merlin Way. DE11 15 G5
Merrydale Rd. DE15 12 A1
Mervin Rd. DE15 8 B4
Meynell Clo. DE15 8 B6
Meynell St. DE11 17 G3
Mickleton Clo. DE11 17 H2
Middle Clo. DE11 14 C3
Midland Rd. DE11 14 D4
Midway Rd. DE11 15 E3
Mill Clo. DE11 15 E3
Mill Hill Dri. DE15 8 B3
Mill Hill La. DE11 8 B3
Millers La. DE14 3 B1
Millersdale Clo. DE15 8 B3
Millfield Croft. DE11 14 C1
Millfield St. DE11 15 H5
Milton Av. DE11 15 E2
Milton St. DE14 3 B2
Moat Bank. DE15 8 D5
Moat St. DE11 14 C6
Moira Rd. DE11 15 F6
Mona Rd. DE13 6 D2
Monarch Clo. DE13 5 F4
Monsaldale Clo. DE15 8 B3
Montpellier Clo. DE14 10 C2
Moor St. DE14 3 A2
Moor Furlong. DE13 5 G4
Moores Clo. DE13 7 E1
Morleys Hill. DE13 4 A4
Mosley St. DE14 3 B2
Mount Pleasant Rd. DE11 17 E4
Mount Rd, Bretby. DE15 9 G4
Mount Rd, Castle Gresley. DE11 16 D3
Mount Rd, Woodville. DE11 15 H4
Mount St. DE15 8 B4
Mountbatten Clo. DE13 5 E5

Napier St. DE14 3 A4
Needwood St. DE14 7 E4
Nelson St, Swadlincote. DE11 14 D3
Nelson St, Winshill. DE15 8 C4
Nene Clo. DE15 4 D1
Neville Clo. DE13 4 D2
New Rd, Newhall. DE11 14 D2
New Rd, Woodville. DE11 15 G4
New St, Burton on T. DE14 3 B4
New St, Church Gresley. DE11 14 D6
Newbury Dri. DE13 4 D1

Wheatbreach Clo. DE13 7 E2
Wheatlands. DE11 14 C1
Wheatlands Rd. DE11 11 H3
Wheatley La. DE15 8 C3
Wideshaft. DE11 15 E3
Wilcock Rd. DE14 10 D2
William Nadin Way. DE11 13 E6
William St. DE14 7 F2
Willow Clo. DE11 14 A1
Willow Dri. DE11 14 B1
Willow Pl. DE15 11 G2
Wilmot Rd. DE11 14 C4
Winchcombe Dri. DE15 8 B6
Winchester Dri, Burton on T. DE14 11 E2
Winchester Dri, Linton. DE12 16 D6
Winchester Dri, Midway. DE11 15 F2
Windmill St. DE11 14 C6
Windsor Clo. DE11 14 C1
Windsor Dri. DE11 8 A6
Windsor Rd. DE12 16 D6
Winster Grn. DE11 14 A3
Wolfscote Dale. DE11 14 A6
Wood Ct. DE14 3 B4
Wood Farm La. DE11 15 F4
Wood La. DE11 13 F2
Wood St, Burton on T. DE14 3 B4
Wood St, Church Gresley. DE11 14 C5
Woodbine Clo. DE14 10 B3
Woodfield Dri. DE11 14 D2
Woodhouse St. DE11 15 E5
Woodland Rd. DE15 12 B4
Woods La. DE15 12 A1
Woodview Rd. DE15 12 D4
Woodville Rd. DE11 15 H4
Woodward Way. DE11 15 F3
Woodwards Pl. DE11 14 D5
Woosnam Clo. DE14 10 D3
Worcester Rd. DE15 11 G3
Wordsworth Av. DE11 15 E2
Wordsworth Dri. DE15 7 F1
Worthington Wk. DE14 3 D2
Worthington Way. DE14 3 C2
Wren Clo. DE11 15 G4
Wye Dale. DE11 14 A6
Wyggeston St. DE13 7 E1
Wyndham Cres. DE15 8 D4

Yard Clo. DE11 14 C4
Yew Tree Cres. DE15 11 H3
Yewtree Rd. DE11 14 B1
York Clo. DE11 15 E2
York Rd. DE11 14 C6
York St. DE14 7 E3

ASHBY-DE-LA-ZOUCH

Abbey Clo. LE65 18 A2
Abbey Dri. LE65 18 A2
Abbotsford Rd. LE65 18 D3
Alton Way. LE65 18 D4
Ashby Ct. LE65 18 B4
Astley Way. LE65 18 E2
Atkinson Rd. LE65 18 B4
Avenue Rd. LE65 18 B4
Baker Av. LE65 18 C3
Bamburgh Clo. LE65 18 C3
Bath St. LE65 18 C3
Beaumont Av. LE65 18 A3
Beech Way. LE65 18 E2
Belvoir Dri. LE65 18 C3
Benenden Way. LE65 18 B2
Berwick Rd. LE65 18 B4
Bowker Cres. LE65 18 A4
Brendon Way. LE65 18 C4
Bridge Pl. LE65 18 C2
Bristol Av. LE65 18 A4
Brittany Av. LE65 18 B2
Brook St. LE65 18 C2

Brown Ct. LE65 18 A2
Burton Rd. LE65 18 A1
Cambrian Way. LE65 18 C4
Canterbury Dri. LE65 18 B2
Castle Way. LE65 18 B4
Cedar Clo. LE65 18 B2
Cheltenham Dri. LE65 18 B1
Chiltern Rise. LE65 18 C4
Churchill Clo. LE65 18 A2
Clifton Dri. LE65 18 B2
Clipton Clo. LE65 18 B1
Coalfield Way. LE65 18 F2
Coniston Gdns. LE65 18 D4
Cotswold Way. LE65 18 C4
Cromwell Clo. LE65 18 E1
Denstone Clo. LE65 18 A1
Derby Rd. LE65 18 B2
Derwent Gdns. LE65 18 D4
Discovery Way. LE65 18 E1
Donnington Dri. LE65 18 A3
Downside Dri. LE65 18 B1
Dunbar Way. LE65 18 D3
Dyson Clo. LE65 18 B1
Elford St. LE65 18 C2
Elm Av. LE65 18 E2
Elvaston Clo. LE65 18 D3
Ennerdale Gdns. LE65 18 D4
Eton Clo. LE65 18 B1
Excelsior Rd. LE65 18 F2
Fairfax Clo. LE65 18 D2
Featherbed La. LE65 18 E1
Ferrers Clo. LE65 18 A3
Fettes Clo. LE65 18 B1
Glenalmond Clo. LE65 18 A1
Grange Clo. LE65 18 B4
Griffith Gdns. LE65 18 A4
Hackett Clo. LE65 18 B2
Hailebury Av. LE65 18 A1
Harrow Clo. LE65 18 B1
Hastings Way. LE65 18 D4
Highfields Clo. LE65 18 A3
Highgate. LE65 18 A1
Hill St. LE65 18 B2
Holywell Av. LE65 18 B1
Holywell Ter. LE65 18 C2
Huntingdon Ct. LE65 18 C2
Huntingdon Rd. LE65 18 A3
Ingle Dri. LE65 18 A2
Ingles Hill. LE65 18 A1
Ivanhoe Dri. LE65 18 A2
Kelso Clo. LE65 18 D3
Kenilworth Dri. LE65 18 C3
Kilburn Rd. LE65 18 F2
Kilwardby St. LE65 18 B3
King George Av. LE65 18 B1
Knights Clo. LE65 18 D2
Leicester Rd. LE65 18 E3
Leith Clo. LE65 18 A2
Locksley Clo. LE65 18 A2
Lockton Clo. LE65 18 D2
Lodge Clo. LE65 18 B4
Loudoun Way. LE65 18 A3
Lower Church St. LE65 18 C2
Lower Packington Rd. LE65 18 C4
Loweswater Gro. EL65 18 D4
Malvern Cres. LE65 18 B1
Manor Clo. LE65 18 B3
Market St. LE65 18 C3
Marlborough Way. LE65 18 B1
Matthews Ct. LE65 18 A2
Melrose Dri. LE65 18 D3
Mendip Clo. LE65 18 C4
Mill La. LE65 18 C2
Millbank. LE65 18 C2
Millfield Clo. LE65 18 B1
Moira Rd. LE65 18 A3
Money Hill. LE65 18 C1
Morton Walk. LE65 18 A4
Mount Walk. LE65 18 D3
Musson Dri. LE65 18 A4
Naseby Dri. LE65 18 E2
North St. LE65 18 C2
Northfields. LE65 18 D2
Nottingham Rd. LE65 18 D2
Oakham Gro. LE65 18 B1

*Oakley Ct, Burton Rd. LE65 18 B2
Oundle Clo. LE65 18 A1
Packington Nook La. LE65 18 B4
Paris Clo. LE65 18 B2
Park Clo. LE65 18 B4
Park Rd. LE65 18 C1
Paulyn Way. LE65 18 A3
Pennine Way. LE65 18 C4
Pentland Rd. LE65 18 D3
Pine Clo. LE65 18 E2
Pithviers Clo. LE65 18 B3
Prestop Dri. LE65 18 A2
Prior Park Rd. LE65 18 C3
Priorfields. LE65 18 D3
Range Rd. LE65 18 D2
Ratcliffe Clo. LE65 18 B2
Rennes Clo. LE65 18 B2
Repton Clo. LE65 18 B1
Resolution Rd. LE65 18 E1
Ridgway Rd. LE65 18 A4
Rockingham Clo. LE65 18 C3
Roedean Clo. LE65 18 B1
Rossall Rd. LE65 18 B1
Rotherwood Dri. LE65 18 B1
Rouen Way. LE65 18 B2
Rowena Dri. LE65 18 B1
Rugby Clo. LE65 18 B1
Rydal Gdns. LE65 18 D4
St Michaels Clo. LE65 18 D4
Saxon Way. LE65 18 A2
Scott Clo. LE65 18 B2
Sherborne Dri. LE65 18 B2
Smedley Clo. LE65 18 A4
Smisby Rd. LE65 18 B1
Smoke Rd. LE65 18 F2
South St. LE65 18 C3
Staley Av. LE65 18 A4
Station Rd. LE65 18 B3
Stone Clo. LE65 18 B1
Stuart Way. LE65 18 C4
Sycamore Dri. LE65 18 D2
Tamworth Rd. LE65 18 A4
The Callis. LE65 18 B2
The Croft. LE65 18 E3
The Gables. LE65 18 D4
The Green. LE65 18 C2
Thirlmere Gdns. LE65 18 D4
Toulouse Pl. LE65 18 B2
Tower Gdns. LE65 18 B3
Trinity Clo. LE65 18 B2
Trinity Ct. LE65 18 B2
Tudor Clo. LE65 18 C4
Tutbury Clo. LE65 18 D3
Ulleswater Cres. LE65 18 D4
Union Pass. LE65 18 C3
Upper Church St. LE65 18 D2
Upper Packington Rd. LE65 18 D4
Uppingham Dri. LE65 18 B2
Warwick Way. LE65 18 C3
Wells Rd. LE65 18 A4
Western Clo. LE65 18 B4
Westfields Av. LE65 18 B4
Westfields Ter. LE65 18 A2
Westminster Way. LE65 18 B1
Wilfred Garden. LE65 18 B3
Wilfred Pl. LE65 18 B3
Willesley Clo. LE65 18 A4
Willesley Gdns. LE65 18 A4
Willesley La. LE65 18 A4
Willowbrook Clo. LE65 18 C1
Winchester Way. LE65 18 B2
Windermere Av. LE65 18 D4
Windmill Clo. LE65 18 D4
Windsor Rd. LE65 18 C4
Wood St. LE65 18 B2
Woodcock Way. LE65 18 D2
Woodside. LE65 18 A3
Wrekin Clo. LE65 18 C4

BARTON-UNDER-NEEDWOOD

Arden Rd. DE13 20 B2

Ash Tree Rd. DE13 20 B2
Aspen Rd. DE13 20 C3
Bar La. DE13 20 A3
Barton Gate. DE13 20 A1
Barton Lodge. DE13 20 C2
Beech Rd. DE13 20 C3
Bell La. DE13 20 B1
Brookside Rd. DE13 20 B2
Captains La. DE13 20 B2
Cedar Rd. DE13 20 C2
Church La. DE13 20 B2
Collinson Rd. DE13 20 B2
Crowberry La. DE13 20 B2
Dogshead La. DE13 20 A3
Dunstall Rd. DE13 20 B2
Efflinch La. DE13 20 C2
Fallowfield Rd. DE13 20 B1
Fullbrook Av. DE13 20 C3
Gilmour La. DE13 20 C2
Green La. DE13 20 A3
Holland Park. DE13 20 B2
Holly Rd. DE13 20 B2
Lichfield Rd. DE13 20 D3
Lindon Rd. DE13 20 B2
Main St. DE13 20 A1
Manor Ct. DE13 20 C1
Meadow Rise. DE13 20 C2
Mill Cres. DE13 20 C3
Mill La. DE13 20 C3
Needwood Pk. DE13 20 C2
Oak Rd. DE13 20 B2
Padhurst Rise. DE13 20 B2
Palmer Clo. DE13 20 C1
Park Clo. DE13 20 A2
Park Rd. DE13 20 A1
Saffron Clo. DE13 20 A2
St James Ct. DE13 20 B1
St James St. DE13 20 B2
St Lukes Rd. DE13 20 B2
Sandiway. DE13 20 C3
Short La. DE13 20 B2
Station Rd. DE13 20 C2
The Alders. DE13 20 A2
The Green. DE13 20 A3
Thornhill Clo. DE13 20 A1
Wales La. DE13 20 B2
Westmead Rd. DE13 20 B2
Willow Rd. DE13 20 B3

REPTON

Askew Gro. DE65 20 B5
Boot Hill. DE. DE65 20 B4
Brook End. DE65 20 B5
Brookside Clo. DE65 20 B5
Broomhills La. DE65 20 B6
Burdett Way. DE65 20 C5
Burton Rd. DE65 20 A5
Chestnut Way. DE65 20 A5
Fisher Clo. DE65 20 B5
Forge Clo. DE65 20 B6
High St. DE65 20 B5
Hill View. DE65 20 C5
Longlands. DE65 20 C5
Main St. DE65 20 B6
Meadow Clo. DE65 20 C5
Milton La. DE65 20 B4
Mitre Dri. DE65 20 B5
Monsom La. DE65 20 B4
Mount Pleasant. DE65 20 C6
Mount Pleasant Rd. DE65 20 C6
Pinfold Clo. DE65 20 C5
Pinfold La. DE65 20 B5
Richmond Ct. DE65 20 C5
Saxon Croft. DE65 20 C5
Shakespeare Clo. DE65 20 C6
Springfield Rd. DE65 20 C5
Stratford Clo. DE65 20 C6
Tanners La. DE65 20 A4
The Crescent. DE65 20 B5
The Pastures. DE65 20 B5
Well La. DE65 20 B6
Willington Rd. DE65 20 A4
Wystan Ct. DE65 20 C5

TUTBURY/HATTON

Appletree Rd. DE65 19 C
Babbington Clo. DE13 19 C
Belmot Rd. DE13 19 B
Birch Gro. DE65 19 D
Bourne Clo. DE13 19 B
Bradshaw. DE65 19 B
Bridge St. DE13 19 C
Brook Clo. DE65 19 C
Burton Rd. DE13 19 C
Burton St. DE13 19 C
Castle Ct. DE13 19 C
Castle Hayes La. DE13 19 A
Castle St. DE13 19 C
Castle View. DE65 19 B
Chatsworth Dri. DE13 19 C
Church Av. DE13 19 D
Church St. DE13 19 C
Close Bank Walk. DE13 19 C
Coopers Croft. DE65 19 C
Cornmill Balk. DE13 19 D
Cornmill La. DE13 19 C
Cromwell Clo. DE13 19 C
Derby Rd. DE65 19 D
Dove Side. DE65 19 C
Duke St. DE13 19 C
Eaton Clo. DE65 19 D
Elm La. DE13 19 B
Fauld La. DE65 19 A
Ferrers Av. DE13 19 B
Field Av. DE65 19 C
Fishpond La. DE13 19 B
Flax Croft. DE65 19 C
Granville Clo. DE65 19 C
Green La. DE13 19 C
Hanbury Av. DE13 19 D
Hassall Rd. DE65 19 D
Heath Way. DE65 19 C
High St. DE13 19 B
Hillcrest. DE13 19 B
Hillside. DE13 19 B
Holme Clo. DE65 19 B
Holts La. DE13 19 B
Hoon Rd. DE65 19 D
Ironwalls La. DE13 19 C
Jinny Clo. DE65 19 C
Lancaster Dri. DE13 19 C
Ley Croft. DE65 19 C
Lime Gro. DE13 19 D
Lower High St. DE13 19 C
Ludgate St. DE13 19 C
Malthouse La. DE65 19 D
Marston La. DE65 19 C
Marston Old La. DE65 19 C
Mercia Clo. DE65 19 C
Monk St. DE13 19 C
Netherclose La. DE65 19 A
Norman Rd. DE13 19 B
Oakwood Clo. DE65 19 B
Park La. DE13 19 B
Peters Ct. DE65 19 D
Pinfold Clo. DE13 19 B
Portway Dri. ED13 19 B
Priory Clo. DE13 19 B
Queens Rise. DE13 19 B
Redhill La. DE13 19 B
Rolleston La. DE13 19 D
Rushton Clo. DE13 19 B
Rye Flats La. DE65 19 D
Sawpit La. DE13 19 B
Scropton La. DE13 19 A
Scropton Old Rd. DE65 19 C
Silkmill La. DE13 19 C
Station Rd. DE65 19 C
The Close. DE13 19 C
The Hays. DE65 19 C
The Park Pale. DE13 19 C
The Shielings. DE65 19 C
Tutbury By-Pass. DE13 19 C
Uttoxeter Rd. DE13 19 B
Wakefield Av. DE13 19 B
Woodmans Croft. DE65 19 C
Yew Tree Rd. DE65 19 C